# The
# WINE
# TRIVIA
## Game Book

# "Penicillin cures, but wine makes people happy."

—ALEXANDER FLEMING

# What you need

- This book!
- 2-6 players
- Scoring method (Pen and paper, or smartphone)

# How to play

Choose a person to keep score.

General trivia questions are worth 1, 2 or 3 points based on difficulty. The youngest player reads the first question to the player directly to his or her right. If the player answers correctly, he or she earns the number of points for that question. (Correct answers can be found on the page that follows each question.) The youngest player passes the book to the person on his or her left, who then asks the next question to the youngest player. Continue moving the book around your group in this fashion.

If only two players, simply pass the book back and forth. You may also choose to play in two teams instead of as individuals.

If a player lands on a bonus round page, that person or team will have an opportunity to earn up to 6 points. Read all instructions aloud when landing on a bonus round page. The question reader should keep track of correct answers in a bonus round, and tally the points for the scorekeeper.

The player or team with the most points at the end wins. You may choose to play the entire book. For a shorter round, elect to end the game on page 50 or page 100, and pick up from there next time.

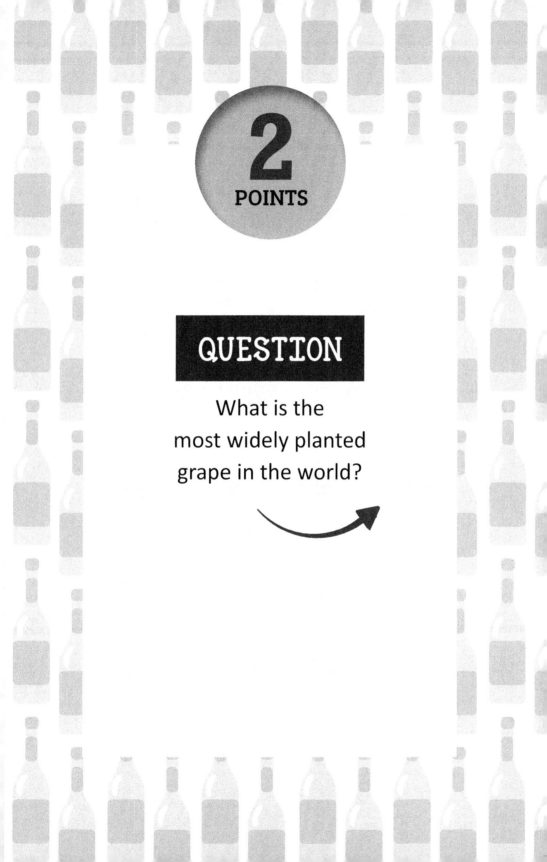

# 2
## POINTS

## QUESTION

What is the
most widely planted
grape in the world?

## ANSWER

Cabernet sauvignon
(*More than 700,000 acres
worldwide*)

**2**
**POINTS**

## QUESTION

What varietal is
Australia's biggest export?

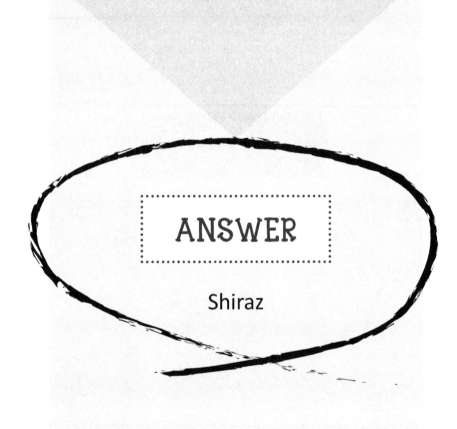

ANSWER

Shiraz

**2 POINTS**

## QUESTION

What is the dominant
grape in chianti?

Sangiovese
(*Italy's most planted
wine grape.*)

**3**
POINTS

## QUESTION

How many grapes does
it take to make a standard
bottle of wine?

*(Answer may be in number of
grapes, or pounds of grapes.)*

## ANSWER

About 200 grapes,
or 2.5 pounds of grapes

**3 POINTS**

## QUESTION

On average, how many gallons
of wine does one acre
of grapevines produce?

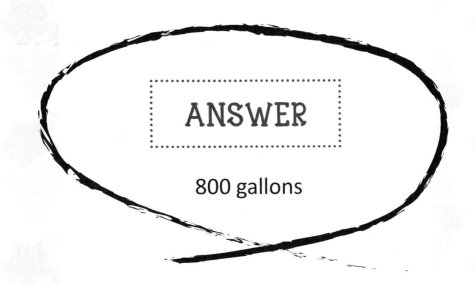

ANSWER

800 gallons

**1**

POINT

## QUESTION

True or false: There are typically about 50,000 bubbles in one bottle of Champagne.

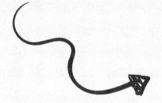

False
(*There are about
49 million bubbles.*)

**1**
POINT

## QUESTION

True or false:
Wine can be blue.

True!
(*Blue wine is fermented from
a mix of red and white grapes,
with added pig-ments.*)

**2**
POINTS

**QUESTION**

Which country has the largest area of vineyards?

Spain
*(About 1,154,000 hectares.)*

**2**
POINTS

## QUESTION

What is the ideal storage
temperature for all wine?

ANSWER

55 degrees Fahrenheit

# BONUS
## Round!

**(Don't wine about it.)**

# BONUS Round!

UP TO

**6**

**POINTS**

Name the top six wine-producing countries in the world.
You may guess six total countries.
(One point for each correct country for a maximum of 6 points.)

**Italy**

**France**

**Spain**

**United States**

**Argentina**

**Chile**

## QUESTION

How many miles per hour can the cork fly out of a Champagne bottle?

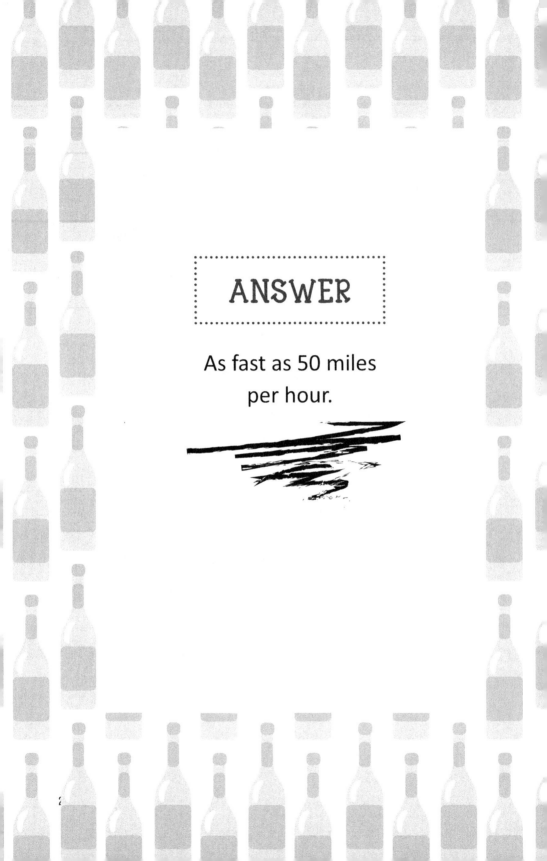

ANSWER

As fast as 50 miles
per hour.

**3**
POINTS

QUESTION

The oldest winery in the world
dates back to 4100 BC.
In what country is it located?

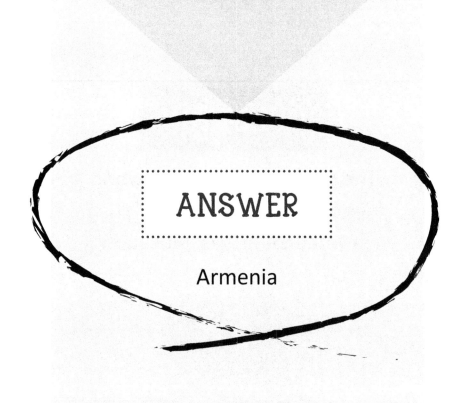

ANSWER

Armenia

**2 POINTS**

## QUESTION

George Washington and
what other U.S. president
attempted – and failed – to
grow grapevines in Virginia?

ANSWER

Thomas Jefferson

## QUESTION

What does non-vintage
(or NV) mean?

It means the wine blend was made of grapes from several different years.

**2 POINTS**

**QUESTION**

What grape accounts
for 23 percent of Germany's
vineyards?

ANSWER

Riesling

**2 POINTS**

## QUESTION

What country
is sherry from?

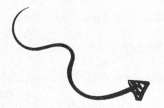

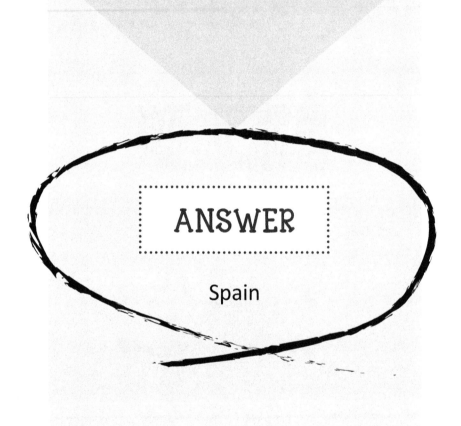

ANSWER

Spain

**QUESTION**

True or false: Grape vines
go dormant in the winter.

## ANSWER

True!

**1**
POINT

**QUESTION**

True or false: Champagne can be made using both red and white grapes.

# ANSWER

True!

## QUESTION

What does it mean if a wine is described as "hot"?

That it's high
in alcohol content.

**3**
POINTS

## QUESTION

What grape is used to
make Prosecco?

ANSWER

Glera

# BONUS
## Round!

(Wine not?)

# BONUS Round!

**UP TO**

# 6
## POINTS

Name that grape! Read the descriptions aloud below one at a time. For each, guess which wine grape is being described.
One guess per description.
(One point for each correct answer for a maximum of 6 points.)

| | |
|---|---|
| Apple, pineapple, citrus, butter, pear, butterscotch, melon, fig. Also, possibly oak, toast, vanilla. | **Chardonnay** |
| Lemon, citrus, gooseberry, grass, green olive. | **Sauvignon Blanc** |
| Cherry, berries, earth, leather, rose. | **Pinot Noir** |
| Currant, blackberry, cedar, eucalyptus, bell pepper. | **Cabernet Sauvignon** |
| Plum, raspberry, dark cherry, chocolate, tobacco, tea. | **Merlot** |
| Raspberry, strawberry, spice, pepper. | **Syrah/Shiraz** |

## 2 POINTS

## QUESTION

Originally associated with France, which grape is used to make most of the red wines in Argentina?

# ANSWER

Malbec

**2 POINTS**

## QUESTION

Which country consumes
the largest volume of wine
in the world?

ANSWER

United States

**3**
POINTS

## QUESTION

What is the name of the science dedicated to the study and knowledge of wines?

## Oenology

**3 POINTS**

## QUESTION

Which wine was used to toast the signing of the Declaration of Independence?

**2 POINTS**

**QUESTION**

How many years after planting is a grapevine ready to make wine?

ANSWER

3 years

**2**
POINTS

QUESTION

In which country was the
corkscrew invented?

## ANSWER

England
(*The first reference to a corkscrew appeared in a museum catalog of 1681.*)

**2**
POINTS

## QUESTION

Which two grapes make up
most wines of Bordeaux?

## ANSWER

Cabernet sauvignon
and merlot

## QUESTION

How old should an oak tree be
to be used as a barrel
for aging wine?

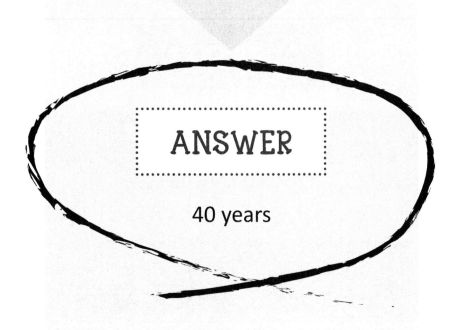

ANSWER

40 years

## QUESTION

True or false: Women were
not allowed to drink wine in
Ancient Rome.

ANSWER

True

# 1
## POINT

## QUESTION

True or false: The most expensive wine bottle sold at auction went for just over $1 million.

## ANSWER

False
(*The most expensive bottle
sold for $558,000.*)

## 3 POINTS

## QUESTION

What is the name of the tall jar that was used to store wine in ancient Greek and Roman society?

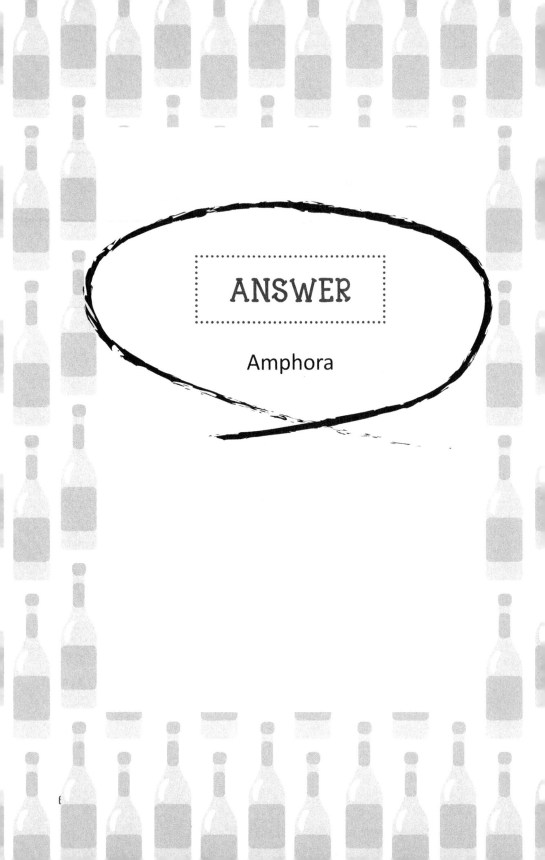

# ANSWER

Amphora

## 3
POINTS

## QUESTION

Who is the official patron
saint of winemakers?

ANSWER

Saint Vincent

**2 POINTS**

## QUESTION

What does a vertical
wine tasting mean?

## ANSWER

The term used when tasting wines all from the same vineyard or winemaker, but from different years.

*(In a horizontal wine tasting, you taste several wines made in the same year.)*

**2**
POINTS

## QUESTION

What type of wine is port?

```
ANSWER
```

Fortified wine
(*Which means it has brandy
or another spirit added to a
wine base.*)

## QUESTION

True or false: Wine is fat
and cholesterol free?

ANSWER

True!

**1**
POINT

## QUESTION

True or false: Wine is
50 percent water.

False

*(Wine is 80-90 percent water.)*

## QUESTION

Who painted the picture
"Red Vines in Arles"?

# ANSWER

Vincent Van Gogh

## POINTS

What 20th century novelist said, "My only regret in life is that I didn't drink more wine"?

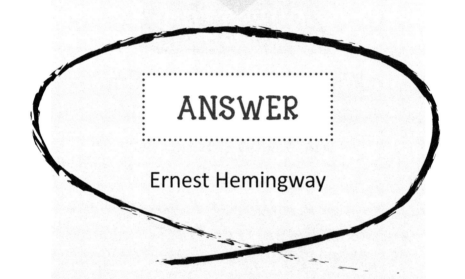

ANSWER

Ernest Hemingway

# BONUS
## Round!

(Read between the wines.)

# BONUS Round!

UP TO

# 5

## POINTS

Wines are often referred to as "Old World" or "New World," depending on where they were made and what wine making traditions are used there. Old World wine is usually lighter in body, and has lower alcohol, higher acidity, and more minerality. New World wine is typically fuller body, and has higher alcohol, lower acidity, and fruit flavors.
Read each country aloud below, and choose if the ones from that country are considered "Old World" or "New World."
(One point for each correct answer for a maximum of 5 points.)

Portugal .........................**Old World**

China .............................**New World**

Australia .........................**New World**

Germany.........................**Old World**

South Africa ...................**New World**

**3 POINTS**

## QUESTION

If you have Novinophobia,
you have a fear of what?

## ANSWER

Running out of wine

**3**
POINTS

## QUESTION

What was the occupation
of Dom Perignon when he
invented Champagne?

**ANSWER**

A monk

# 2
## POINTS

## QUESTION

In addition to the levels
of tannins, which factor
determines a dry white wine?

# ANSWER

Acidity

**2**
POINTS

## QUESTION

The color of wine is
determined by which part
of the grapes?

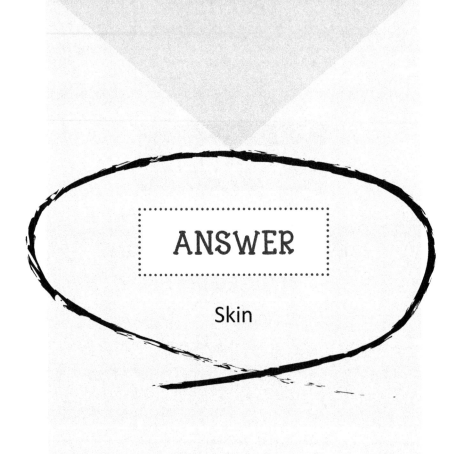

ANSWER

Skin

## QUESTION

Retsina is a type of wine coming from which country?

# ANSWER

## Greece

## QUESTION

Which famous scientist
found out that yeast would
trigger fermentation?

ANSWER

Louis Pasteur

# BONUS
## Round!

(Chardon-hey!)

# BONUS Round!

**UP TO**

# 5
## POINTS

Name the five U.S. states that had the highest wine consumption in 2020. You may take five total guesses. (One point for each correct answer for a maximum of 5 points.)

**California** (*156, 032 gallons*)

**Florida** (*80,742 gallons*)

**Texas** (*64,370 gallons*)

**New York** (*63,613 gallons*)

**Illinois** (*38,510 gallons*)

## QUESTION

What causes a vanilla flavor
in wine?

## ANSWER

The age of the barrel
(*If newer oak barrels were
used, the wines often have a
hint of vanilla in both aroma
and flavor.*)

**2**
POINTS

Why are rose trees typically
planted close to vineyards?

They can be an early warning
system for certain types of fungi
that can affect the grapevines.

**2**
**POINTS**

**QUESTION**

The oldest recorded evidence
for using grapes in a wine
recipe comes from which
country?

ANSWER

China

**2**

POINTS

What does the term
"Demeter" mean on the label
of wine bottles?

## ANSWER

Biodynamic wine

## QUESTION

True or false: Red wine becomes darker over time.

## ANSWER

False
(*It becomes lighter.*)

**1**
POINT

## QUESTION

True or false: White wine
becomes darker over time.

## ANSWER

True!

## 2 POINTS

What are vineyards called
in South Africa?

# ANSWER

## Wine farms

## POINTS

**QUESTION**

Most wines should be consumed within how many years after being bottled?

## ANSWER

Within 5 years
*(Only around 10% of wine benefit
from more aging.)*

**3**
POINTS

## QUESTION

What does "plonk" mean
when discussing wine?

## ANSWER

A British slang term
used to refer to cheap,
low-quality wine.

**QUESTION**

The oldest known wine cellar
was discovered where?
(Hint: It was not on dry land.)

On the Titanic
(*When divers discovered the wreckage, most of the bottles were still intact.*)

## QUESTION

Screw caps on wine bottles were popularized in Australia and what other country?

ANSWER

New Zealand

## 2 POINTS

## QUESTION

What country is the world's
leading cork producer?

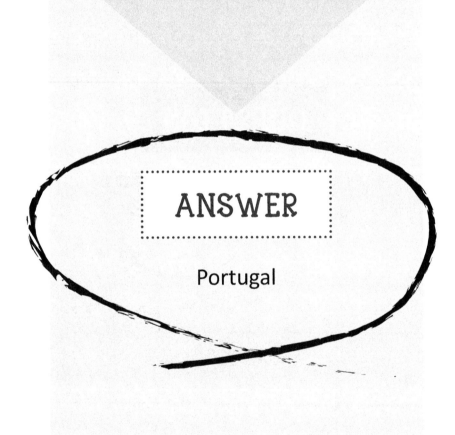

ANSWER

Portugal

## QUESTION

True or false: Wine bottles
are best stored with the cork
pointing straight down.

False
(*Horizontal storage is best. This allows the cork to keep damp and prevents excess air from entering the bottle.*)

**1**
POINT

**QUESTION**

True or false:
Every U.S. state has a winery.

## QUESTION

How many known grape
varieties are there
in the world?

ANSWER

10,000

**2**
POINTS

## QUESTION

One grape cluster equals
how many glasses of wine?

## ANSWER

One

## QUESTION

When is National Wine Day
in the United States?

# ANSWER

May 25

**2 POINTS**

## QUESTION

What is the most planted grape variety in California?

## ANSWER

Chardonnay

## QUESTION

The oldest bottle of wine was
found in Germany.
What year was it from?

ANSWER

325 A.D.

## QUESTION

What toxic substance did ancient Romans mix with wine because they thought it helped preserve it?

## ANSWER

Lead

**2**
POINTS

## QUESTION

What 1990s songwriter sung about a black fly in your chardonnay?

ANSWER

Alanis Morrisette

## POINTS

### QUESTION

What two women were
known for drinking wine on
their morning talk show?

141

## ANSWER

Kathie Lee Gifford
and Hoda Kotb

# BONUS
## Round!

(Some you wine, some you lose.)

# BONUS Round!

UP TO

# 5
## POINTS

Test your wine language skills! Read each language aloud below.
For each, say "wine" in that language.
(One point for each correct answer for a maximum of 5 points.)

Italian.................. **Vino**

France................ **Vin**

Portuguese ......... **Vinho**

Greek.................. **Κρασί (krasi)**

Hungarian........... **Bor**

## QUESTION

How many glasses of orange juice would you need to drink to get the same amount of antioxidants in one glass of wine?

## ANSWER

Seven
(*And you would need
to drink 20 glasses
of apple juice!*)

## 2 POINTS

## QUESTION

Pantone's 2009 color of the
year was named after what
sparkling wine cocktail?

## ANSWER

Mimosa

## QUESTION

In the 2004 film "Sideways," Paul Giammati's character Miles refuses to drink what wine varietal?

# ANSWER

## Merlot

## QUESTION

What Hollywood couple helped create a wine called "Quarantine" and donated 100 percent of the proceeds to COVID-19 relief charities?

## QUESTION

How many calories does a
5-ounce glass of wine contain?

# ANSWER

About 105 for red,
and 100 for white.
(*Either answer is correct.*)

## QUESTION

Where did the Zinfandel
grape originate?

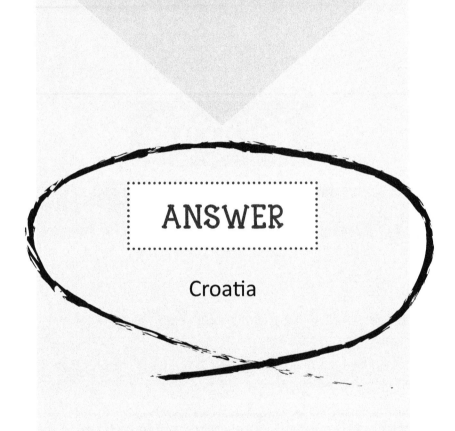

ANSWER

Croatia

## QUESTION

What is the name of the process used primarily in making red wine that involves steeping grape skins to extract color, tannins and aroma?

### ANSWER

Maceration

**3**
POINTS

## QUESTION

What is the wire cage on a
Champagne bottle called?

A muselet,
which comes from the
French word meaning
"to muzzle."

# BONUS
## Round!

(On cloud wine.)

# BONUS Round!

UP TO

# 5
## POINTS

Read each country below aloud. For each, state what term is used for sparkling wine in that country. One guess per location. (One point for each correct answer for a maximum of 5 points.)

Spain................... **Cava**

Portugal .............. **Espumante**

South Africa ........ **Méthode Cap Classique (or Cap Classique)**

Germany............. **Sekt**

Hungary .............. **Pezsgő**

## QUESTION

What term is used for the
fragrance of old wine?

ANSWER

Mellow

**3**
POINTS

## QUESTION

What champagne
is preferred
by James Bond?

## ANSWER

Bollinger

## QUESTION

What city in the United States boasts the most wine consumed per person?

Washington, D.C.,
with an average of almost
seven gallons consumed
per person per year.

**2 POINTS**

## QUESTION

How does rosé wine
get its pink color?

The skin of red grapes is
immersed in the wine for
a short amount of time.

## QUESTION

What country
produces rioja wine?

ANSWER

Spain

**2**
POINTS

## QUESTION

What country produces
Barolo wine?

ANSWER

Italy

**2 POINTS**

## QUESTION

What type of wine
did Marilyn Monroe
famously bathe in?

# ANSWER

Champagne

**2**
POINTS

## QUESTION

What gives sparkling wine the right to be called Champagne?

It must come from the
Champagne region of France.

## QUESTION

What is the name of the
bubble trains that travel up
the side of a glass?

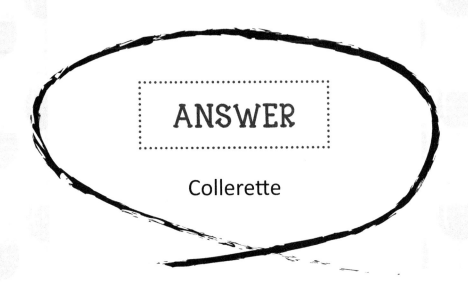

# ANSWER

## Collerette

## QUESTION

What does the French word
"chambre" mean?

Room temperature

**2 POINTS**

## QUESTION

What vessel is used to serve wine that also allows it to breathe?

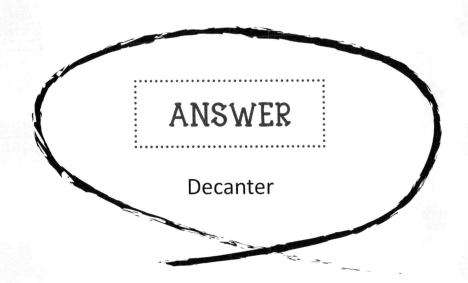

ANSWER

Decanter

## QUESTION

What word describes
a dry champagne?

## ANSWER

Brut

## QUESTION

How many gallons of wine
are in a barrel?

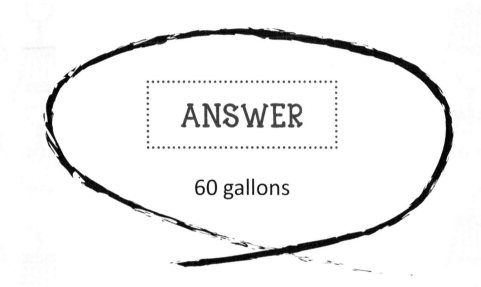

ANSWER

60 gallons

**2**
POINTS

Which country is home
to Gallo, the world's largest
wine producer?

## ANSWER

United States

**2 POINTS**

## QUESTION

What country produces
Lambrusco wine?

# ANSWER

## Italy

# 2
## POINTS

**QUESTION**

Why should you hold
a wine glass by the stem?

## ANSWER

So your hand does not affect
the temperature of the wine.

# 2
## POINTS

## QUESTION

Grapes used to make sweet
wine or dessert wine have
a higher what?

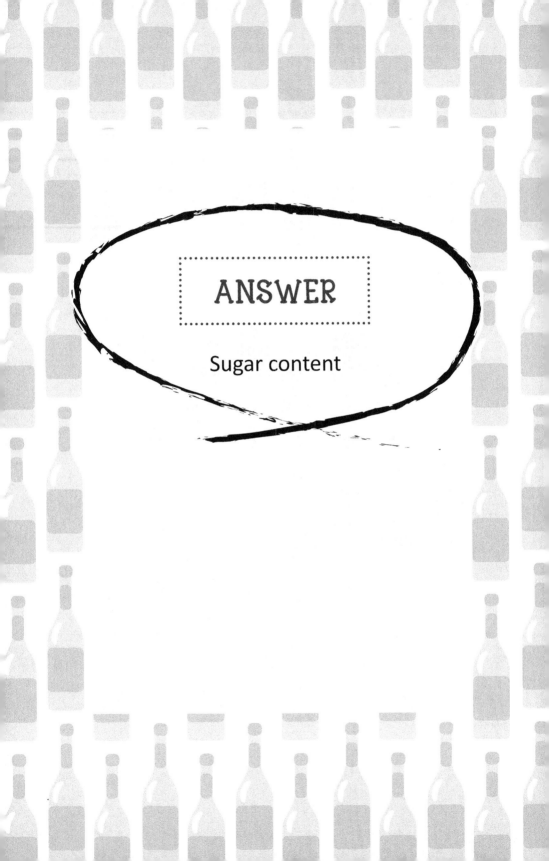

# ANSWER

Sugar content

## QUESTION

True or false: Champagne bottles are made from thicker glass than wine bottles.

True!
*(Thicker glass is used to resist the pressure from carbonation.)*

## QUESTION

True or false:
Wines produced in colder
climates are usually sweeter.

## ANSWER

False
(*Warmer climate wines
are sweeter.*)

**2 POINTS**

## QUESTION

Why is the glass used
for wine bottles often tinted?

## ANSWER

To protect the wine from light

## QUESTION

When wine drinkers say they're in the "ABC Club," what do they mean?

## ANSWER

That they'll drink
"Anything But Chardonnay."

# "Wine is bottled poetry."

—ROBERT LOUIS STEVENSON

# Thank you!

The purchase of this book supported
a small business owner. We hope you enjoyed it!

Printed in Great Britain
by Amazon

33950754R00116